Piano/Vocal Arrangements by Maury Yeston

Titanic logo design by Doug Johnson, © 1997
Production photography by Joan Marcus

Original cast recording available on **RCA VICTOR** 09026-68834-2/4

For a comprehensive listing of Cherry Lane Music's songbooks, sheet music, instructional materials, videos
and more, check out our entire catalog on the Internet. Our home page address is: http://www.cherrylane.com

WHITE STAR LINE

TITANIC

Dodger Endemol Theatricals
Richard S. Pechter
The John F. Kennedy Center for the Performing Arts

present

TITANIC

A New Musical

Story and Book by
Peter Stone

Music and Lyrics by
Maury Yeston

Featuring
(in alphabetical order)

Adam Alexi-Malle   Becky Ann Baker   Melissa Bell   Matthew Bennett   Judith Blazer   John Bolton
Jonathan Brody   Bill Buell   Michael Cerveris   Victoria Clark   Mindy Cooper   Allan Corduner
David Costabile   Alma Cuervo   John Cunningham   Brian d'Arcy James   Lisa Datz   David Elder
David Garrison   Jody Gelb   Kimberly Hester   Erin Hill   Robin Irwin   John Jellison
Peter Kapetan   Larry Keith   Joseph Kolinski   Theresa McCarthy   Drew McVety
Martin Moran   Michael Mulheren   Stephanie Park   Jennifer Piech   Michele Ragusa
Ted Sperling   Mara Stephens   Don Stephenson   Henry Stram
Andy Taylor   Clarke Thorell   Kay Walbye   William Youmans

Scenic and Costume Design
Stewart Laing

Lighting Design
Paul Gallo

Sound Design
Steve Canyon Kennedy

Orchestrations
Jonathan Tunick

Music Supervision and Direction
Kevin Stites

Music Coordinator
John Miller

Casting
Julie Hughes & Barry Moss, CSA

Technical Supervisor
Aurora Productions

Action Coordinator
Rick Sordelet

Production Stage Manager
Susan Green

Executive Producer
Dodger Management Group

Press Representative
Boneau/Bryan-Brown

Marketing Consultant
Margery Singer

Associate General Manager
Robert C. Strickstein

Choreographed by
Lynne Taylor-Corbett

Directed by
Richard Jones

Photos

Pp. 2–3: Top: Capt. E. J. Smith, Architect Thomas Andrews, Owner J. Bruce Ismay. Insets: "What A Remarkable Age," "How Did They Build Titanic?," "I Must Get On That Ship." Bottom: "Doing The Latest Rag." P. 4: Act 1 Finale. P. 5: "Lady's Maid." P. 6: "The Blame." P. 7: "Still."

CONTENTS

In addition to winning the Tony Award for Best Score for *Titanic*, Maury Yeston also won the Tony and two Drama Desk Awards for his music and lyrics to Broadway's *Nine* (which won five other Tonys including Best Musical and was nominated for a Grammy Award and London's Olivier Award). His work on Broadway's *Grand Hotel* was also nominated for a Tony and two Drama Desk Awards.

Yeston's lyrics and music cover a variety of styles. His Cello Concerto was premiered by Yo Yo Ma, while his album *Goya—A Life In Song* featured Placido Domingo and Gloria Estefan and included the song "Till I Loved You,"—subsequently a Top 40 Barbra Streisand hit. The classical crossover *December Songs* was commissioned by Carnegie Hall for its centennial celebration and recorded on RCA Records. Other Yeston works recorded on RCA Records include the score to his *Phantom*, which has received national and international acclaim, and the London Concert version of *Nine,* which starred Jonathan Pryce and Elaine Paige.

Yeston holds a BA and MA from both Yale University and Clare College, Cambridge, as well as a Ph.D. from Yale, where he was a member of the faculty for eight years as the Director of Undergraduate Studies in Music.

IN EVERY AGE

Music and Lyrics by Maury Yeston

Stately ♩. = 92

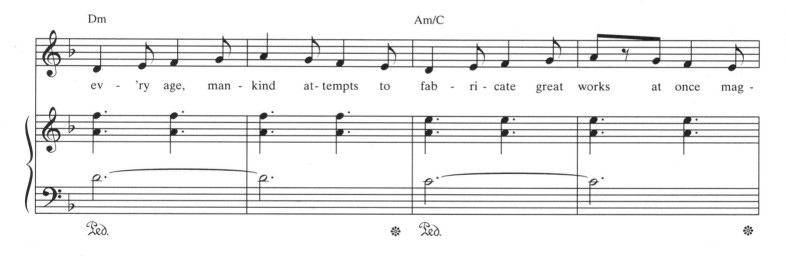

ev - 'ry age, man - kind at - tempts to fab - ri - cate great works at once mag -

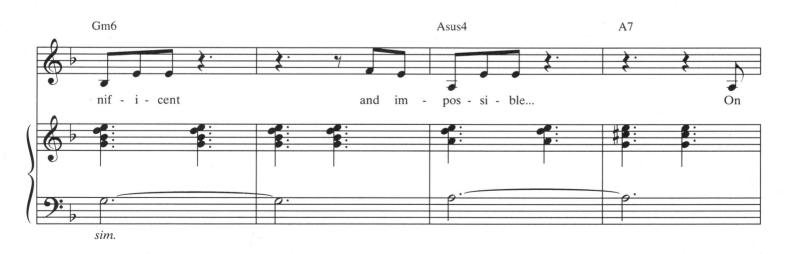

nif - i - cent   and im - pos - si - ble...   On

sim.

HOW DID THEY BUILD TITANIC?

Music and Lyrics by Maury Yeston

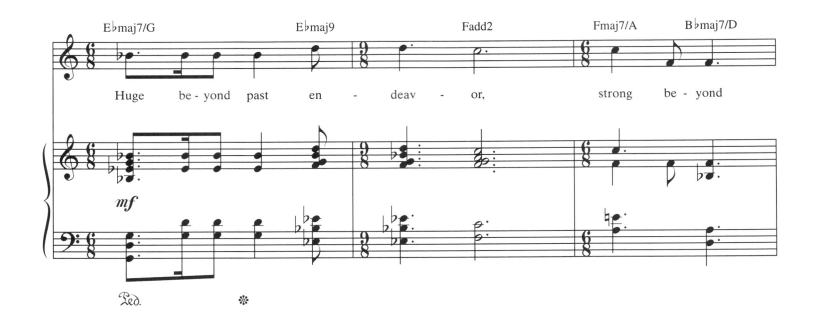

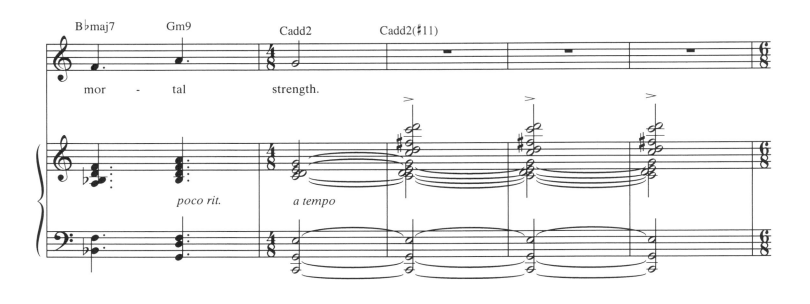

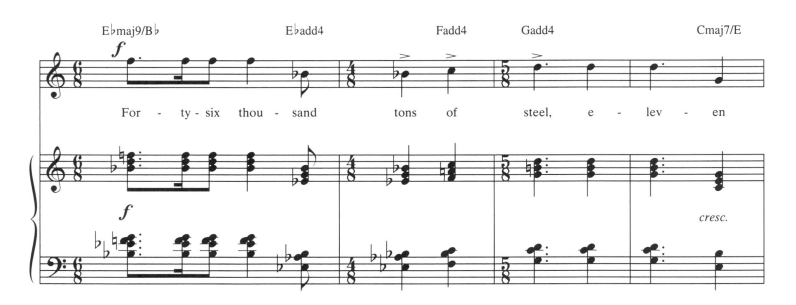

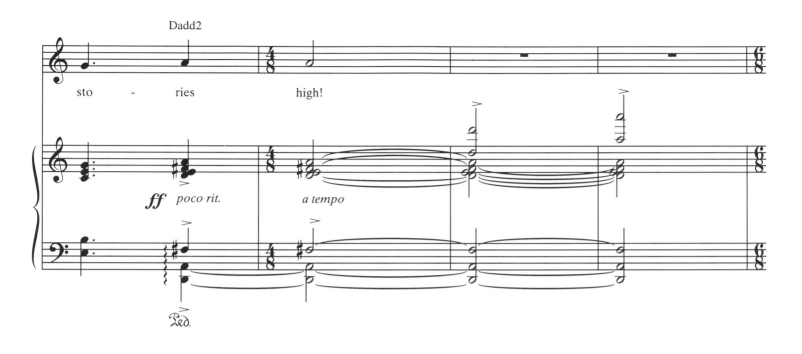

sto - ries   high!

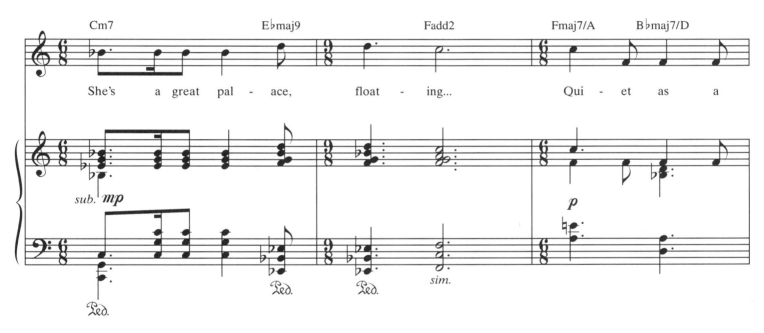

She's   a   great pal - ace,   float - ing...   Qui - et   as   a

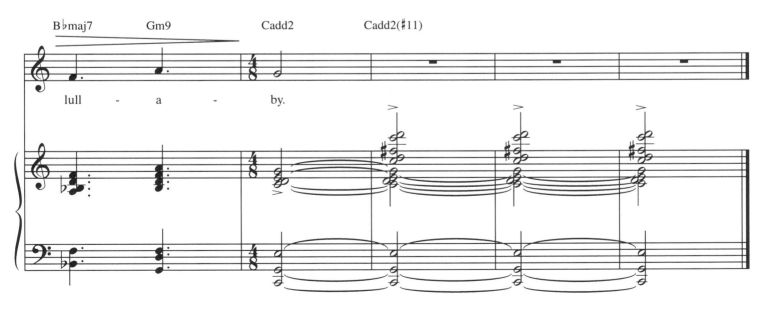

lull - a -   by.

THERE SHE IS

Music and Lyrics by Maury Yeston

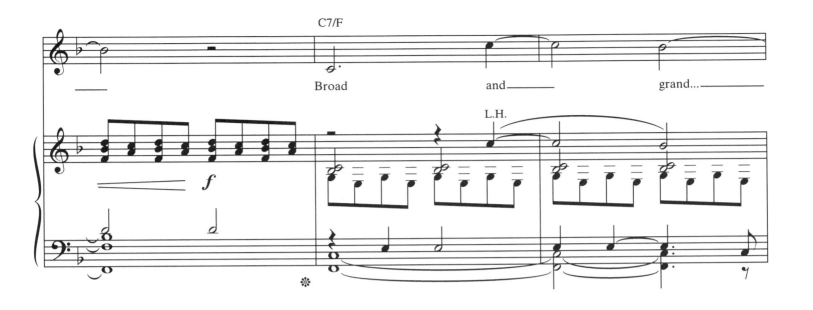

Broad and grand...

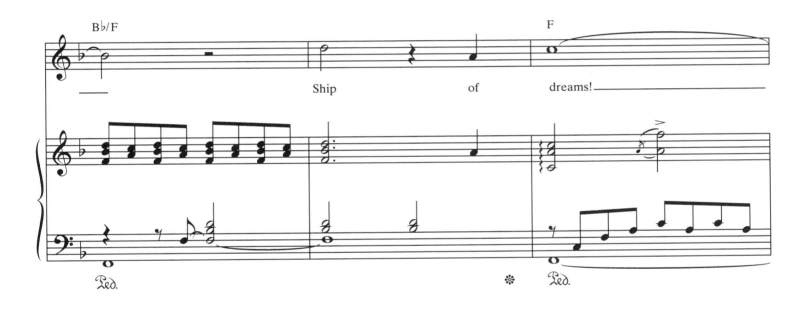

Ship of dreams!

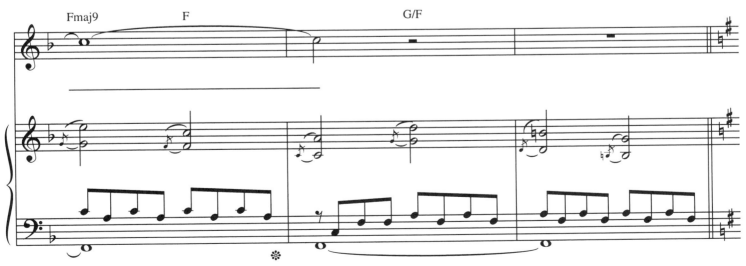

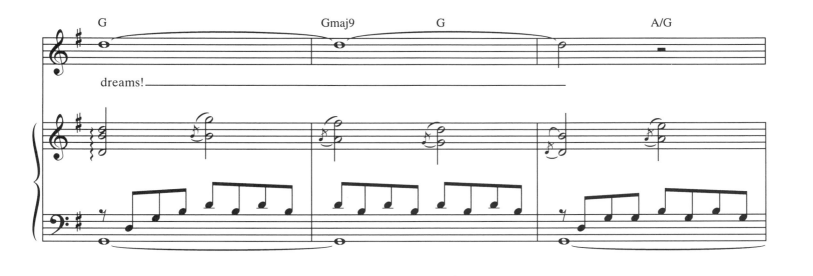

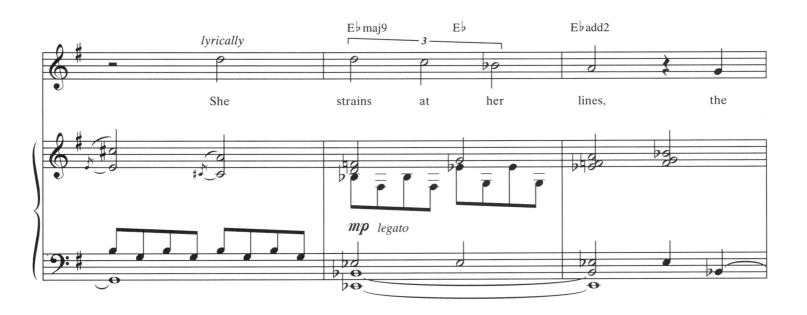

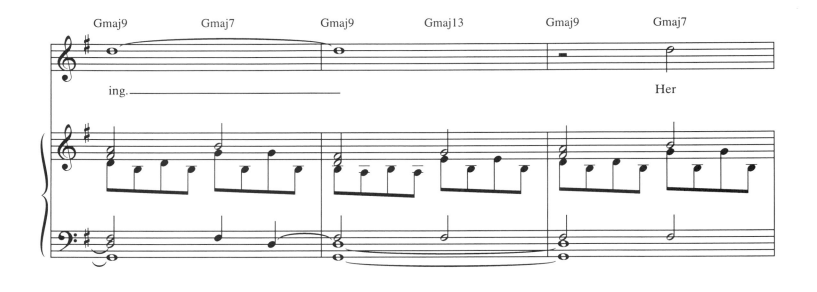

ing. ———————————————————— Her

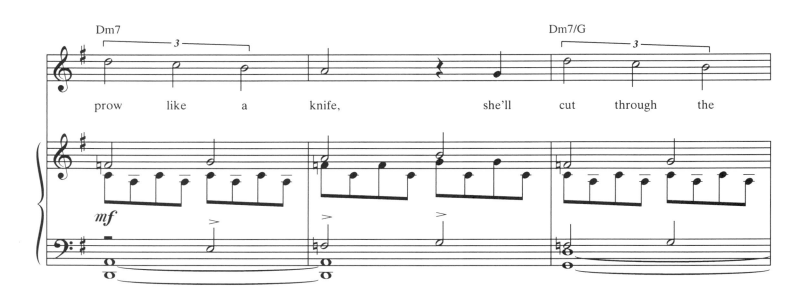

prow like a knife, she'll cut through the

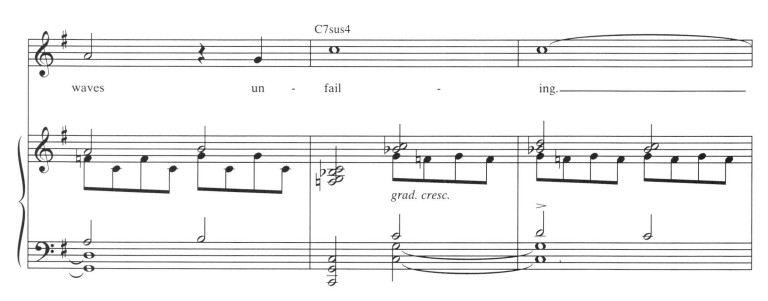

waves un - fail - ing. ——————————

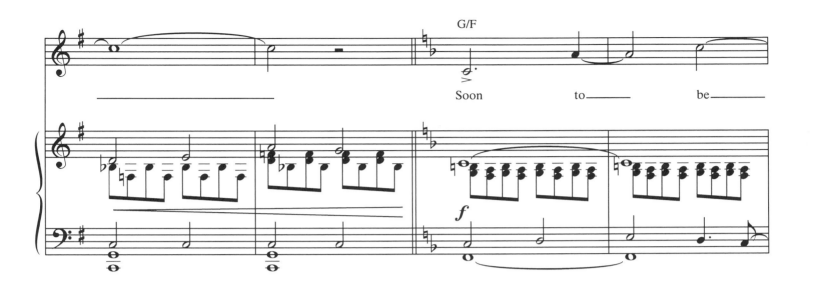

Soon to be

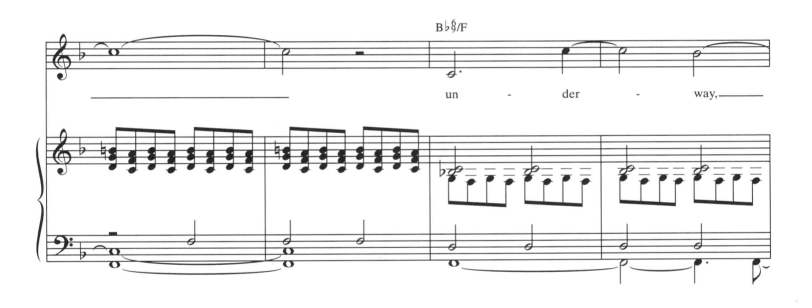

un - der - way,

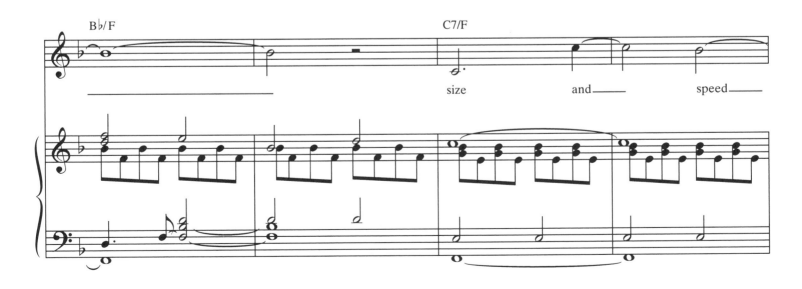

size and speed

un - ex - plored...

And I'll be a - board that

ship____ of

dreams!

I Must Get on That Ship

Music and Lyrics by Maury Yeston

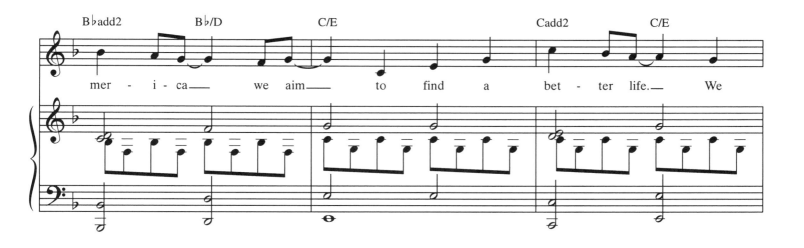

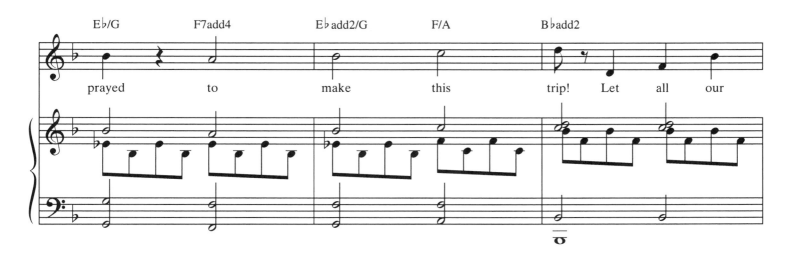

served a berth__ to be a - board.__ Now point me toward__ that__ ship!__

The fin - est peo - ple will at - tend; the best a - mong them we'll be - friend.__ They'll stand right next to us,__ be at my

fin - ger - tip! Great heads of state and mil - lion - aires

— who run the world's af - fairs— will all be there.— I

must get on— that— ship! For the maid - en

voy - age! For the maid - en voy - age!

Get us all a - board.

Tempo I (♩ = 84)
Broadly, and with nobility

Lift up the ramp,— let go the lines,— raise up her

col - ors and— de - signs!— Pre - pare— for cast - ing off,— and

through the port we'll slip! Each per - son

Godspeed Titanic (Sail On)

Music and Lyrics by Maury Yeston

molto rit.

ry   me._____   Sail

on,_____   sail   on,_____   great   ship_____

_____   Ti - tan - ic._____   Cross_____   the

o - pen   sea!_____

For - tune's winds sing God - speed to thee!

Barrett's Song

Music and Lyrics by Maury Yeston

Coal it is that makes the steam that runs the ma - chines that run the world that sends the men be - low the ground to mine the

coal_____ each

day._____

From Leices - ter - shire and Not - ting - ham,__ us lads who worked down

in the pit__ knew if you got a - bove the ground__ you'd save_____ your

born to the coal, there's no place_____ for you_____ else-

where._____ You

trade a life of dank and gloom to shov-el in the boil-er room. But

now you're sev-en decks be-low a la - dy's dain -

ty feet!_____ And noth-ing has changed. There's noth-ing a min-er can do._____ The pit and your mates turned in-to the hold and the crew._____

WHAT A REMARKABLE AGE

Music and Lyrics by Maury Yeston

With great excitement ♩. = 126

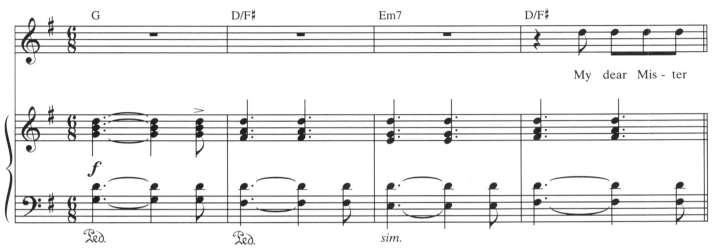

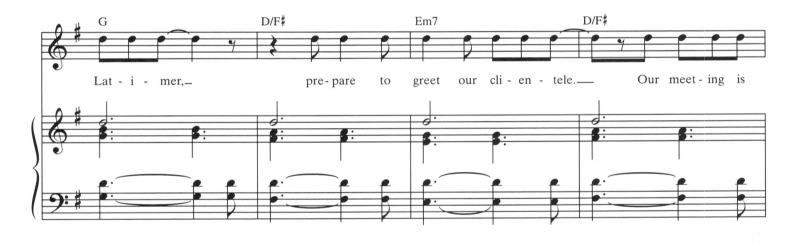

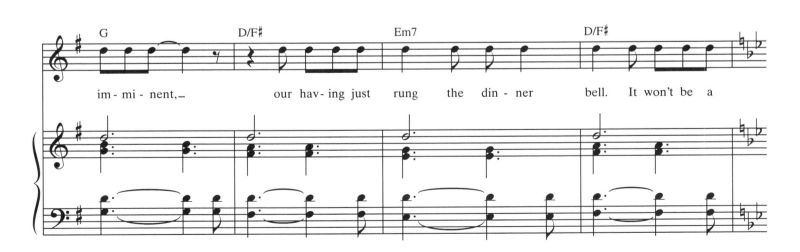

As - tor takes his toast dry!
Cap - tain's ta - ble pris - tine!

Mis - sus Strauss likes the
Here we seat the e -

grouse with the sauce on the side!
lite whom we hap - pi - ly serve!

And the Wide - ners love kid - ney
Here they dine on fine French cui -

pie!
sine!

Bring it hot. If it's not, they'll be fit to be tied!
It's the crème de la crème's ex - clu - sive pre - serve!

They're ac - cus - tomed to the best of all that mon - ey buys....
It's the pleas - ure of the lei - sure class - 's great - est wits

The world of free en-ter-prise— has giv-en this priv-'lege to the rich! When they're
to be where the Cap-tain sits— when tak-ing his din-ner on the sea! Giv-ing

i-dle they're en-ti-tled to the lux-u-ry— which we pro-vide that's for-
def-'rence to their pref-'renc-es is our chief art!— We play a part in a

ev-er the source of our pride!————— Which is why we're al-ways
per-fect-ly work-ing ma-chine!————— You should ev-er be a-

there with our es-pe-cial form of care for ev-'ry hun-gry mil-lion
ware this is a priv-'lege great and rare, a spe-cial bur-den that we

TO BE A CAPTAIN

Music and Lyrics by Maury Yeston

Prayer-like ♩ = 80

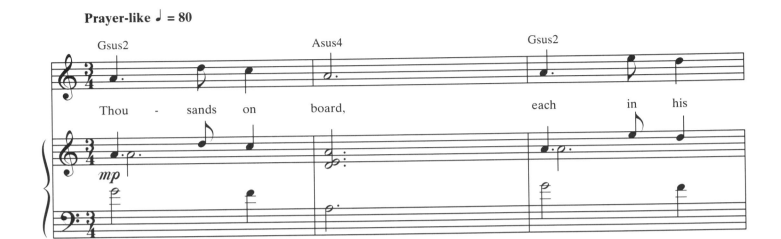

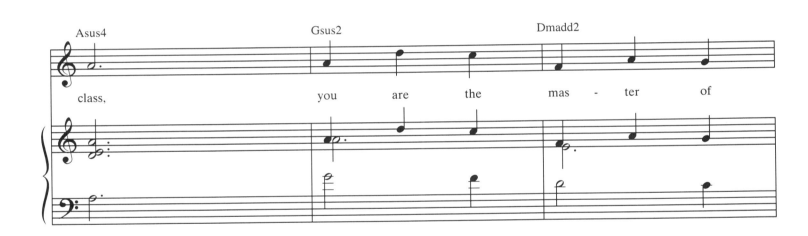

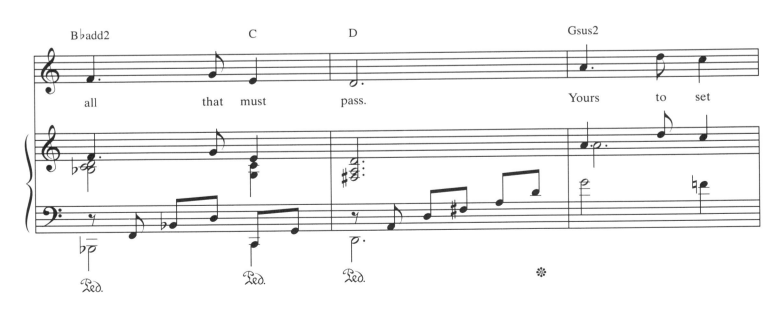

LADY'S MAID

Music and Lyrics by Maury Yeston

In that grand - est na - tion I'll stand tall,___

reach my ver - y high - est hopes of all.___

Dreamily ♩ = 88

I want to be a

la - dy's maid, la - dy's maid in A - mer - i - ca.

I've seen it on the map. There's a place in A-mer-i-ca called Al-ber-kew-kew, and I'm hop-in' it's a bit like Don-e-gal. Oh, I'm hop-in' that it is.

There, I'm hop-in' that it is. Where my dream-in' and my

hop-in' and my schem-in' and my pray-in' and my wish-in' to be hap-py will come true e-nough and...

cresc. poco a poco

poco rit.

f

Cadd2   G/B Am7

Oh, I   will be

I want to be an en-gi-neer, an en-gi-neer.

a tempo

And I'm plan-ning that it will. How I'm plan-ning that it will. Where my dream-in' and my hop-in' and my schem-in' and my pray-in' and my wish-in' to be hap-py will come true e-nough and I want to be a mil-lion-aire,— mil - lion-aire in A - mer-i - ca!—

Strike it rich and spend the for - tune I a - mass! I want to be a con - sta - ble, con - sta - ble in A - mer - i - ca! In A - mer - i - ca you rise a - bove your class! Oh,

la - dy's maid, en - gi- neer in A - mer - i - ca.

Mil - lion- aire in A - mer - i - ca.

Bet - ter place for me and you. Bet - ter land to start a -

new. *(Show lyric:)* Bet - ter land for the ba -
(Alt. lyric:) Bet - ter land for the new

*A is an alt. melody.

The Proposal

Music and Lyrics by Maury Yeston

Marry me when I return, Dar - lene.

And un - til that day, my love, take care. Be thee

well. May the Lord who watch - es

all watch o - ver thee. May God's

Segue THE NIGHT WAS ALIVE

77

THE NIGHT WAS ALIVE

Music and Lyrics by Maury Yeston

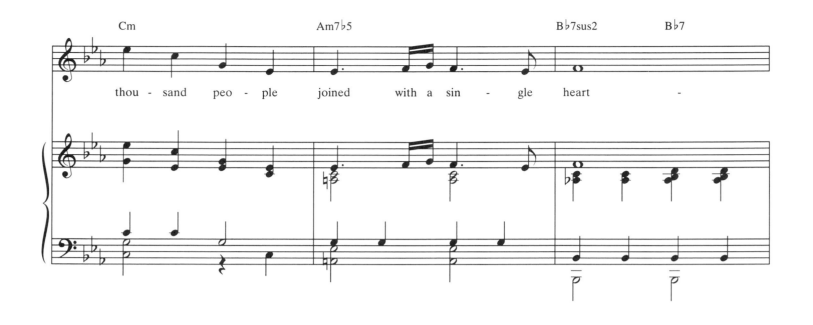

thou - sand peo - ple joined with a sin - gle heart -

beat. Tap - ping out our dit dit dah dit dah dit, dit dit dah dit dah

dit, dit dit dah dit dah ev - 'ry - where.

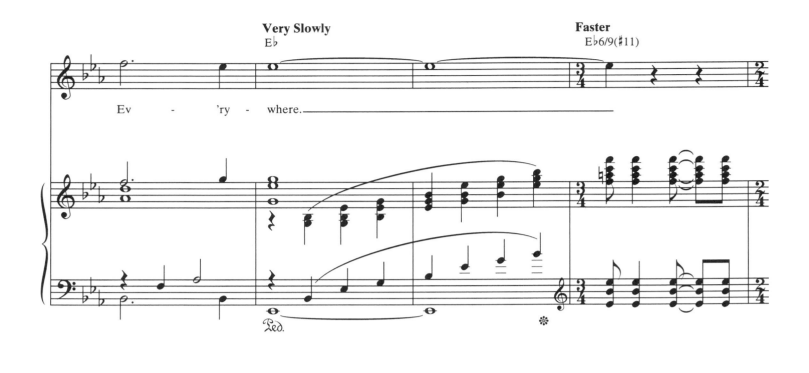

Very Slowly

Ev - 'ry - where.

Faster

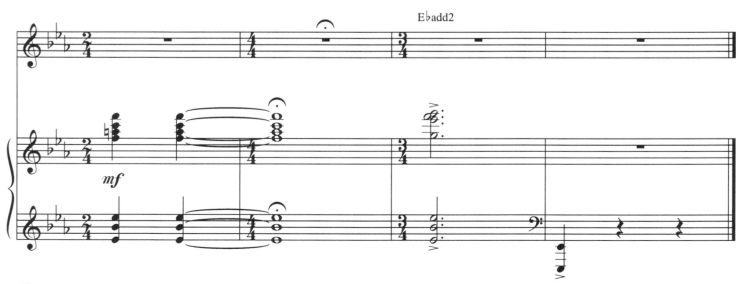

DOING THE LATEST RAG

Music and Lyrics by Maury Yeston

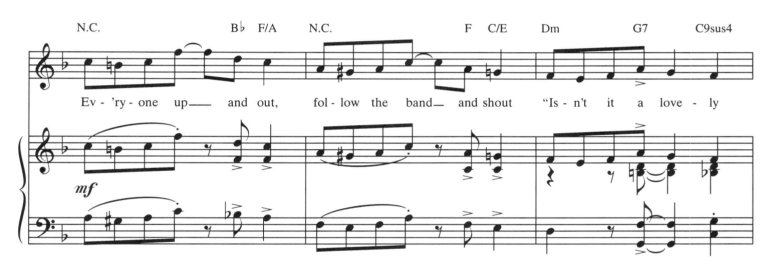

How long since we first— met?— Has it been three days or four?—
It seems like so much long - er
than a lit - tle week - end jag! On the ship by our - selves on this
glo - ri - ous af - ter - noon, do - ing the lat - est rag! I love the

band is bet-ting this rag-time set-ting will take you— a - way!

Ev - 'ry - one up— and out, no - bod - y lag— a - bout, let your dark - er spir - its

climb! Stroll - ing with the or - ches - tra be - side you, play - ing four - four

time. We've got a fel - low who's bet - ter on cel - lo than

an - y oth - er ship can brag! So take your girl by the hand and lend an

ear to the band and do to - day's lat - est rag! Come danc - ing

out on the Well Deck, ship's per - son - nel deck, feel all the o - cean

out on the Well Deck, ship's per - son - nel deck, feel all the o - cean

Ev - 'ry - one is burst - ing with e - mo - tion!

Danc - ing as we cross the might - y o - cean!

Has - n't it been ab - so - lute - ly great to dance the lat - est

rag!

I Have Danced

Music and Lyrics by Maury Yeston

round   us,   Ed - gar!   *Edgar:* Won't   you   ev - er   give

up   that   view?   *Alice:* I   want   more   than   we've

got   now,   Ed - gar...   Why   don't   you?_____

NO MOON

Music and Lyrics by Maury Yeston

AUTUMN

Music and Lyrics by Maury Yeston

Dreamily, in 1 ♩. = 46

Au - tumn. Shall we all meet in the au - tumn? Gold - en and glow - ing, by au - tumn, shall we still be best of

friends?_____ Best of friends...

Au - tumn. Life's bit - ter - sweet in the

au - tumn. New col - ors___ show - ing by

au - tumn. Sum - mer's green mem - o - ry

We'll Meet Tomorrow

Music and Lyrics by Maury Yeston

Steadily building ♩ = 72

We'll meet to-mor-row; we will find a path and reach to-mor-row past this day of

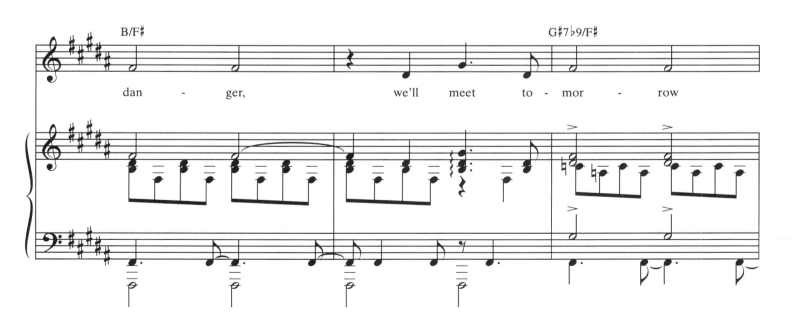

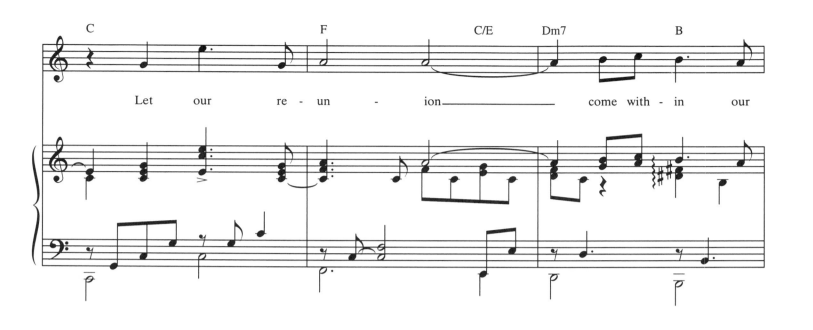

Let our re - un - ion _____ come with - in our

power. Grant one more chance to

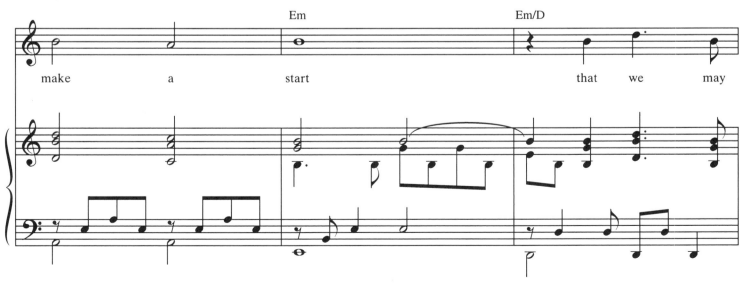

make a start that we may

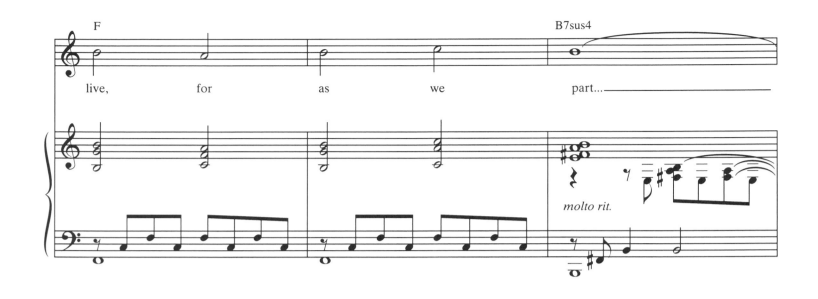

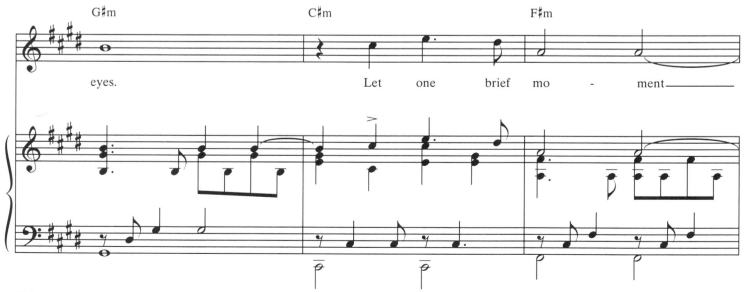

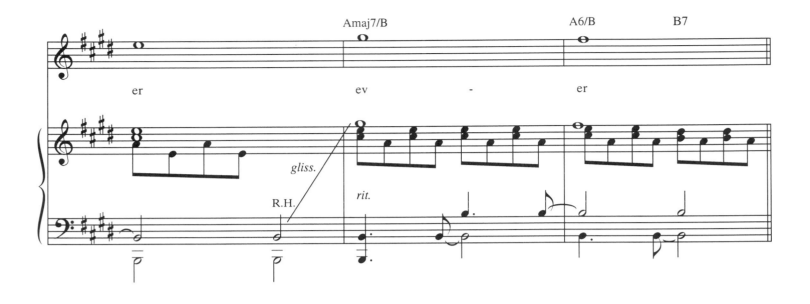

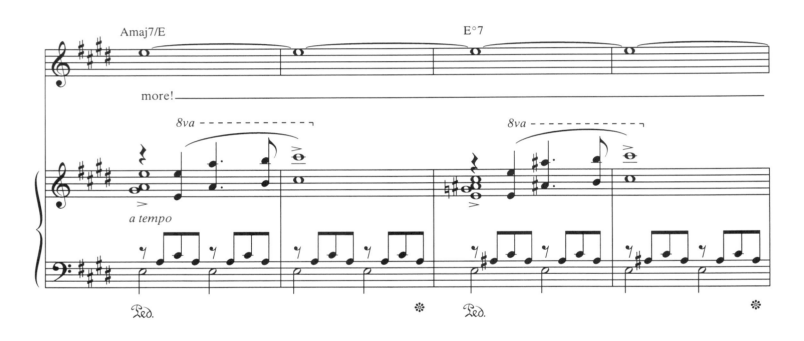

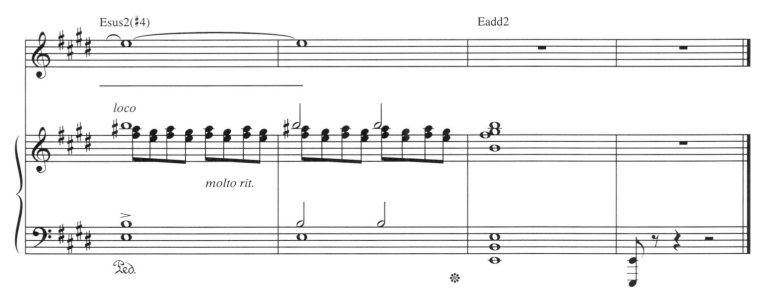

STILL

Music and Lyrics by Maury Yeston

*Cue notes are an alternate melody.

THE MUSIC OF MAURY YESTON

FROM CHERRY LANE MUSIC

NINE
Vocal Selections
02502895

Tony awards for Best Musical and Best Score were just part of the acclaim for this international sensation! Selections include Unusual Way • Guido's Song • Folies Bergeres – and 12 more!

PHANTOM
Vocal Selections
02502105

The delightfully melodic score and stirring story have thrilled audiences across America and Europe. Selections include Melodie de Paris • You Are Music • My True Love • Home – and more!

GRAND HOTEL
Vocal Selections
02507978

Songs from the memorable Tony-award winning musical. Selections include Grand Parade (Theme from Grand Hotel) • At The Grand Hotel • and I Want To Go To Hollywood – plus photos from the acclaimed Broadway production.

DECEMBER SONGS
02502082

Commissioned for the Carnegie Hall centennial season and first performed in 1991, this contemporary song cycle was inspired by Schubert's Winter Journey. Its haunting melodies and richly dramatic writing provides a unique vehicle for the solo singer.

SHEET MUSIC:

GRAND PARADE
02504086

NEW WORDS
02509581

UNUSUAL WAY
02504097

AVAILABLE FROM YOUR LOCAL MUSIC DEALER

Cherry Lane Music

EXCLUSIVELY DISTRIBUTED BY

HAL•LEONARD® CORPORATION

7777 W. BLUEMOUND RD. P.O. BOX 13819 MILWAUKEE, WI 53213